HIS UNIQUENESS, KUI...

Books by David H.J.Gay referred to in this volume:

Christ Is All: No Sanctification by the Law.

Christ's Obedience Imputed.

Eternal Justification: Gospel Preaching to Sinners Marred by Hyper-Calvinism.

Preaching Today: Food for Action as well as Thought.

Public Worship: God-Ordained or Man-Invented?

To Confront or Not to Confront?: Addresses to Unbelievers.

Man

His Uniqueness, Ruin and Redemption

David H.J.Gay

BRACHUS

BRACHUS 2021
davidhjgay@googlemail.com

Scripture quotations come from a variety of versions

To Gabriel, who invited me,
and to the congregation at Pidley Baptist chapel –
the hearers of the original discourses.

Contents

Introduction

In 2021, I was asked to preach three sermons on man – his uniqueness, his ruin and his redemption. As I explained to the congregation, although it was a vital topic that I had been asked to deal with, I was not – to say the least – eager to do it. I like to think of myself as a gospel preacher, and I felt – and still feel – that the material in question would have been better presented as a series of lectures.[1] Nevertheless, despite my reservations, I went ahead and fulfilled the engagement.[2]

About halfway through the process, it crossed my mind that the material might do some good if I published it – slightly expanded – as a booklet. Hence the work in your hand. Only time will tell whether or not my hopes will be realised.

Let me say at once that in what follows you will find nothing scientifically profound. Indeed, I have nothing at all to say on the basis of science. My purpose is to set out the teaching of the Bible – the teaching of the Bible on man – doing so in very brief compass.[3] The fact is – and I want there to be no misunderstanding about this – I openly and unapologetically believe the Bible to be the word of God, and everything I say depends absolutely on that conviction.

But before you dismiss this little work on that account, there are certain things you must bear in mind.

We all have to face and answer some big questions: What is man? Where does he come from? Why is he here? Where is he going?

---

[1] For more on the distinction, see my *Preaching*.
[2] All three discourses are available on my sermonaudio.com page – 'Man's Uniqueness'; 'Man's Ruin'; 'Man's Redemption'.
[3] I underline this. To set out a full explanation of all the points I raise would mean I would have to publish a tome and not a booklet.

Putting it personally: What am I? Where did I come from?[4] Why am I here? Where am I going?

The truth is – and we all need to admit it – in thinking about such questions, no expert in science, philosophy, psychiatry, cosmology, sociology or whatever – however learnèd, however highly qualified he[5] might be in his field, however many prestigious prizes he might have won – can do anything other than I am doing here: namely, set before you his conviction, his belief. What is more, you, too, are a believer: you believe Professor X, you believe theory Y, or whatever. I believe the Bible. As I say, in that conviction, I want to put before you the relevant teaching of the Bible on man – his uniqueness, his ruin and his redemption. Then it will be up to you: you have to decide. But whatever you decide, you will still be a believer, only a believer, and nothing but a believer. I am not for a moment despising academic prowess; I am simply stating an obvious – but often neglected – fact: in this area, we are all believers.

In asserting what the Bible says about God and man – not trying to 'prove' it scientifically – I am following the example set by Paul – and he was no mean academic! Facing the pagan, superstitious, religious intellectuals at Athens, he unapologetically declared:

> What therefore you worship as unknown, this I proclaim to you. The God who made the world and everything in it, being Lord of heaven and earth, does not live in temples made by man, nor is he served by human hands, as though he needed anything, since he himself gives to all mankind life and breath and everything. And he made from one man every nation of mankind to live on all the face of the earth, having determined allotted periods and the boundaries of their dwelling place, that they should seek God, and perhaps feel their way toward him and find him. Yet he is actually not far from each one of us... Being then God's offspring,

---

[4] I am not, of course, thinking of reproduction.

[5] I am using 'he' in the generic sense; that is, both men and women. Indeed, this is a booklet about man; that is, human beings.

we ought not to think that the divine being is like gold or silver or stone, an image formed by the art and imagination of man. The times of ignorance God overlooked, but now he commands all people everywhere to repent, because he has fixed a day on which he will judge the world in righteousness by a man whom he has appointed; and of this he has given assurance to all by raising him from the dead (Acts 17:23-31).

Assertion, assertion, assertion, confident and dogmatic![6]

In order to drive home this vital point, I need to poleaxe a common myth; namely, that Christians, being believers, are gullible, while those who rely on one of the sciences are hard-headed, clear-sighted, no-nonsense people who accept only what can be proved. 'Science has proved...'.

This, of course, is nonsense. Real scientists know that proof is only possible in the realm of mathematics, and that in a very specific and clearly-defined sense: starting with certain axioms, certain fundamental principles, mathematicians build an entire edifice, layer by layer, each succeeding layer resting on what has been established; hence, proof. But physicists, chemists, geologists, cosmologists and the like, can only work on hypotheses[7] and explanations which, though tested by known evidence, and though seeming to explain all known facts, will always be open to correction as more evidence is unearthed. For example, the phlogiston theory, once held to explain the process of burning, was later shown to be false; and Einstein's work on relativity has been updated and tweaked; and so on. The truth is, there is no absolute in science; there can be no absolute in science – it is always a work in progress; today's scientific 'law' is simply the best explanation thus far.[8] Real scientists know and admit this.[9]

---

[6] See my *Confront*.

[7] A hypothesis is 'a supposition or proposed explanation made on the basis of limited evidence as a starting point for further investigation'.

[8] The man in the street uses the word 'law' far too freely – in 'the law of averages', for instance.

Heisenberg's Uncertainty Principle – fundamental to quantum mechanics – embraces all science: 'uncertainty' is the key word.[10]

The point is, the questions I am concerned with here are not susceptible of proof. The existence of God, the origin of life, the meaning of life, and so on, are all matters of belief. The existence of God – or his non-existence – is not a matter of proof; it is a question of belief. Every atheist is a believer every bit as much as any Christian – he believes there is no God. Indeed, in my opinion, it requires a greater faith to believe there is no God than to believe there is.

With that in mind, therefore, let us go on to think about man – his uniqueness, his ruin and his redemption.

---

[9] Alister McGrath: 'All of us, whether atheists or... believers, have to learn to live with uncertainty about those beliefs that we think *really* matter – such as the existence of God, the nature of the good, or the meaning of life. I had to learn to live in a world in which we cannot prove our core convictions' (Alister McGrath: *Through a Glass Darkly: Journeys through Science, Faith & Doubt – a Memoir*, Hodder & Stoughton, London, 2020, viii, emphasis original).

[10] Werner Karl Heisenberg (1901-1976) was a German physicist. Here is one explanation of his Principle: 'Heisenberg's Uncertainty Principle states that there is inherent uncertainty in the act of measuring a variable of a particle... This is contrary to classical Newtonian physics... The Heisenberg Uncertainty Principle is a fundamental theory in quantum mechanics that defines why a scientist cannot measure multiple quantum variables simultaneously. Until the dawn of quantum mechanics, it was held as a fact that all variables of an object could be known to exact precision simultaneously for a given moment. Newtonian physics placed no limits on how better procedures and techniques could reduce measurement uncertainty so that it was conceivable that with proper care and accuracy all information could be defined. Heisenberg made the bold proposition that there is a lower limit to this precision making our knowledge of a particle inherently uncertain'. Today, this principle is widely accepted and used in many areas of study.

* * *

As for my three discourses, when I started to mull over how I should begin, my mind went to David's words in Psalm 8:

> When I look at your heavens [O LORD], the work of your fingers, the moon and the stars, which you have set in place, what is man that you are mindful of him, and the son of man that you care for him? (Ps. 8:3-4).

This is it: What is man? David was clearly lost in wonder about it all. What is man? That was David's burning question – and it had to be mine as I opened this little series. Indeed, I had to do what I could to make it the burning issue for my hearers. And the same applies to you as you read on.

David spoke of two things.

First, the immensity of the universe – as he saw it in the clear night sky – made him think of the smallness of man when compared to that immensity. *What* is man? What *is* man? What is *man*? How much more powerfully should the sheer magnitude of the universe stir us! David, remember, was speaking three thousand years ago. With the passage of those three millennia, how much clearer is our understanding! Take one issue: light years. We know – David did not – that the stars we see tonight are not actually there. That is where each one of them was so many, many years ago (all different). The light from each star has been travelling at 186,000 miles a second to reach us! Numbers here beyond comprehension! With this knowledge, therefore, how much greater than David's should be our sense of wonder at the immensity of the universe, and how much greater our sense of the smallness of man, our smallness.

So much for the first point.

Secondly, and even more amazing, even more wonderful, despite the immensity of the universe – and, therefore, the immensity of God – God cares for man: the infinite cares for the speck.

So said David.

All this is highly relevant today.

Take the first point. We live in a time of the culture of man – man-centred-ness, gross self-centeredness, man's greatness. It is the age of man – the star, the superstar, the big name. And not only on the silver screen or TV, sports field, or in politics, whatever. This culture of man, alas, has permeated the church, fostered by the tyranny of modern means of communication, especially social media.[11] As the world of entertainment has its galaxy of superstars, so the church. In saying this, I do not mean to argue that the culture of the elevation of man is only a recent phenomenon. Certainly not! It was there in apostolic days. Paul had to fight it at Corinth, as both his letters to that *ekklēsia* prove:

> Each one of you says: 'I follow Paul', or 'I follow Apollos', or 'I follow Cephas', or 'I follow Christ' (1 Cor. 1:12).

Consequently, he bluntly observed:

> You are still of the flesh. For while there is jealousy and strife among you, are you not of the flesh and behaving only in a human way? For when one says: 'I follow Paul', and another: 'I follow Apollos', are you not being merely human? (1 Cor. 3:3-4).

---

[11] Think of the revolution in the means of communication: it used to be oral, then by writing, then hand-worked print (what an explosion that was – the Reformation, for instance), then machine-worked print, then radio, then TV (think of how transmission westwards by East German TV, immediately followed by westward transmission by West German TV, led to the fall of the Berlin Wall, 9th Nov. 1989), then digital print, then e-mail, then the internet, and now social media. Think how the latter is responsible for the frequent outbreaks of mass hysteria caused by fake news. Christendom – for ill as well as good – has not remained immune. Believers have yet to reap the full harvest of their widespread use of contemporary, instant mass-communication. The firstfruits look far from promising. Have we reached the stage where, for many evangelicals, Zech. 4:6 has to be rewritten to read: 'Not by might, nor by power, but by social media'?

18

Paul knew he had to prick the bubble. And how!:

> What then is Apollos? What is Paul? Servants through
> whom you believed, as the Lord assigned to each. I planted,
> Apollos watered, but God gave the growth. So neither he
> who plants nor he who waters is anything, but only God
> who gives the growth. He who plants and he who waters are
> one, and each will receive his wages according to his labour.
> For we are God's fellow workers. You are God's field,
> God's building (1 Cor. 3:5-9).

> So let no one boast in men. For all things are yours, whether
> Paul or Apollos or Cephas or the world or life or death or
> the present or the future – all are yours, and you are Christ's,
> and Christ is God's (1 Cor. 3:21-23).

So much for Paul's first salvo across the bows of the *ekklēsia*
at Corinth, in reference to the cult of man. In much of his
second letter, Paul dealt at length with the Corinthian cult of
the so-called 'super apostle'.

With the advent of Christendom,[12] things rapidly spiralled to
giddy heights, and they have never looked back. Within the
evangelical world, the cult of man has never been more
vigorous. It has always been a danger; never more so than
today. As I hinted, the digital revolution is pouring petrol on
the flames. Consequently, we all need constantly to be
reminded of God – his greatness, his care for men – and how
much we depend upon him, and our smallness in his
presence. We need to recover – or discover – a sense of the
wonder of God.

God, in his word, reminds us how brief our life is, how small,
how insignificant, we humans are. Alas, we too often forget
this, and get inflated ideas of ourselves and other men.

In addition to Psalm 8, here are some more salutary words
drawn from the Bible, words which should stop us in our
tracks:

---

[12] Although I have written about this in numerous books, one source
must suffice: see 'Christendom' in my *Relationship*.

My days are swifter than a weaver's shuttle and come to their end without hope. Remember that my life is a breath; my eye will never again see good. The eye of him who sees me will behold me no more; while your eyes are on me, I shall be gone. As the cloud fades and vanishes, so he who goes down to Sheol does not come up; he returns no more to his house, nor does his place know him anymore (Job 7:6-10).

Man who is born of a woman is few of days and full of trouble. He comes out like a flower and withers; he flees like a shadow and continues not (Job 14:1-2).

[God] return[s] man to dust and say[s]: 'Return, O children of man!' For a thousand years in your sight are but as yesterday when it is past, or as a watch in the night. You sweep them away as with a flood; they are like a dream, like grass that is renewed in the morning: in the morning it flourishes and is renewed; in the evening it fades and withers (Ps. 90:3-6).

As for man, his days are like grass; he flourishes like a flower of the field; for the wind passes over it, and it is gone, and its place knows it no more (Ps. 103:15-16).

O LORD, what is man that you regard him, or the son of man that you think of him? Man is like a breath; his days are like a passing shadow (Ps. 144:3-4).

Stop regarding man in whose nostrils is breath, for of what account is he? (Isa. 2:22).

All flesh is grass, and all its beauty is like the flower of the field. The grass withers, the flower fades when the breath of the LORD blows on it; surely the people are grass. The grass withers, the flower fades, but the word of our God will stand forever (Isa. 40:6-8; see 1 Pet. 1:24).

Like a flower of the grass [the rich man] will pass away. For the sun rises with its scorching heat and withers the grass; its flower falls, and its beauty perishes. So also will the rich man fade away in the midst of his pursuits (Jas.1:10-11).

What is your life? For you are a mist that appears for a little time and then vanishes (Jas. 4:14).

And yet, as I say, men so often ignore such truths, and run away with inflated ideas of themselves and others; not least, in the evangelical world. How tragic!

The Dorset poet, William Barnes (1801-1886), superbly captured the proper sense in a poem he penned about himself and his thoughts, under the title 'How Great Do I Become!':

How great do I become! How great!
With all my children now full-grown,
And settled, each a wedded mate,
And all with children of their own.
I first was one, and then one more
Well-wived; and children made me ten;
And they with all their wives or men,
And children, now make me two score,
With children's children, far or nigh,
How great I am become! Am I?

I own a share of Weston folk,
On Norton work I have some hands,
At Beechley I send up a smoke,
My surname sounds on Ashridge lands.
In Meldon church my voices sing,
Yes, there I have young tongues to pray,
And I have boys and girls at play
Below the rocks, at Clevewell spring.
With all the souls that I may claim
How great I am! How great my name!

But oh! how little can I track
The longsome team of father men,
That runs, from me to elders, back
A chain of links beyond my ken.
O'er what dear heads, by one and one,
My name at length came down on me
I know not now, nor may I see
Below me one child's child's sweet son.
No. I am only one of all
Those links of life. But one. How small!

Yes, man is small. But that is not the end of the story – no, not by a long way! Read on!

Man's Uniqueness

God, as he approached the climax of his work of creation, declared:

> Let us make man in our image, after our likeness. And let them have dominion over the fish of the sea and over the birds of the heavens and over the livestock and over all the earth and over every creeping thing that creeps on the earth (Gen. 1:26).

Consequently:

> God created man in his own image, in the image of God he created him; male and female he created them... The LORD God formed the man of dust from the ground and breathed into his nostrils the breath of life, and the man became a living creature (Gen. 1:27; 2:7).

While man is a part of creation, he is more: he is unique within the creation. In particular, man is not just another animal. Only of man did God say: 'Let us make...'. Moreover, only of man did God say: 'Let us make man in our image, after our likeness'. 'So God created man in his own image, in the image of God he created him; male and female he created them'.

Whatever being 'created in God's image' entails, at the very least it means that man is rational, and this certainly marks a vital difference between man and animals. Man is governed by reason, animals by instinct. Man is distinct, unique.

In any case, every part of creation is distinct from every other:

> God gives [every aspect of creation] a body as he has chosen, and to each kind of seed its own body. For not all flesh is the same, but there is one kind for humans, another for animals, another for birds, and another for fish. There are heavenly bodies and earthly bodies, but the glory of the heavenly is of one kind, and the glory of the earthly is of another. There is one glory of the sun, and another glory of

23

the moon, and another glory of the stars; for star differs from star in glory (1 Cor. 15:38-41).

I repeat, therefore, that man is not just another animal; not even the highest animal: 'There is one kind [of body] for humans, another for animals'. But it goes deeper than that, far deeper. It is not just difference in the body: man and the animal have different bodies, yes, but only man – not the animal – is made in the image of God.

Moreover, a vital aspect of God's purpose in creating man was that he should rule the rest of creation: 'Let them have dominion over' it, was God's decree. Thus man is the most privileged part of creation. He is not just another animal. Unique is the word.

Man's Ruin

God, having created man, for man's good, for man's companionship, then formed woman (Gen. 2:18-23). The man and the woman were to live in a state of bliss (Gen. 2:24-25), governed by God's command:

> The LORD God took the man and put him in the garden of Eden to work it and keep it. And the LORD God commanded the man, saying: 'You may surely eat of every tree of the garden, but of the tree of the knowledge of good and evil you shall not eat, for in the day that you eat of it you shall surely die' (Gen. 2:15-17).

Alas, despite this express command with its clear, attendant warning, man fell:

> When the woman saw that the tree [that is, the tree, the fruit of which God had expressly commanded them not to eat] was good for food, and that it was a delight to the eyes, and that the tree was to be desired to make one wise, she took of its fruit and ate, and she also gave some to her husband who was with her, and he ate. Then the eyes of both were opened, and... (Gen. 3:6-7).

That is to say, that, as God had warned the man and the woman, when they sinned by breaking God's commandment, they brought upon themselves the inevitable consequences of which they had been warned. Not only did they come to know that they had sinned, but they felt guilty about it, and, their eyes being opened to their shame, they tried to hide their sin from each other, and from God.

All was vain (Gen. 3:7-14).

As they had been warned, God called them to account and formally pronounced judgment upon them:

> Cursed is the ground because of you; in pain you shall eat of it all the days of your life; thorns and thistles it shall bring forth for you; and you shall eat the plants of the field. By the sweat of your face you shall eat bread, till you return to the

ground, for out of it you were taken; for you are dust, and to dust you shall return (Gen. 3:17-19).

Let me summarise thus far:

Man was created.

Man was created unique.

Man was privileged.

Man was given responsibilities.

Man was placed under the commandment of God.

Man was warned of the consequences of sin, defined as the breaking of God's command.

Man fell – and reaped the consequences: an awakened conscience, a sense of guilt, fear, shame and misery, leading to evasion, attempting to hide from God, but all in vain: Adam and Eve were now under the judgment of a threefold death – immediate spiritual death, eventual physical death, and, if dying unreconciled to God, eternal death.

Moreover man now had to live, not in a paradise, but in a fallen, hostile world. As in Genesis 3:17-19, just quoted, Adam, by his sin, dragged all creation down with him. Thus Paul could speak of:

> ...the sufferings of this present time... For the creation was subjected to futility, not willingly, but because of him who subjected it... [in] bondage to corruption... The whole creation has been groaning together in the pains of childbirth until now (Rom. 8:18-22).

This brings us to the crux, the cardinal issue, in this matter of man's sin. We need to be clear as to how – precisely – Adam's sin affected humanity. Adam fell into sin and ruined himself: he, himself, came under the wrath of God for his sin, yes. But his disobedience and its consequences were far, far more serious and far-reaching than that. Adam's sin had a dire effect on all his posterity, the entire human race:

Sin came into the world through one man [that is, Adam], and death through sin, and so death spread to all men because all sinned... Death reigned... Many died through one man's trespass... Judgment following one trespass brought condemnation... Because of one man's trespass, death reigned through that one man... One trespass led to condemnation for all men... By the one man's disobedience the many were made sinners... Sin reigned in death (Rom. 5:12-21).

By a man came death... In Adam all die... (1 Cor. 15:21-22).

This is the key point. Adam sinned, and by his sin, by that one act of disobedience, he ensured that all his descendants would be constituted accountable sinners under the wrath of God.

What does this mean? How does it show itself?

Paul opened his classic statement of the natural condition of every human being as a sinner under the wrath of God thus:

The wrath of God is revealed from heaven against all ungodliness and unrighteousness of men, who by their unrighteousness suppress the truth (Rom. 1:18).

Because he is a sinner, the natural man 'suppresses the truth'. What truth? Paul spelled it out:

The wrath of God is revealed from heaven against all ungodliness and unrighteousness of men, who by their unrighteousness suppress the truth. For what can be known about God is plain to them, because God has shown it to them. For his invisible attributes, namely, his eternal power and divine nature, have been clearly perceived, ever since the creation of the world, in the things that have been made. So they are without excuse. For although they knew God, they did not honour him as God or give thanks to him, but they became futile in their thinking, and their foolish hearts were darkened. Claiming to be wise, they became fools, and exchanged the glory of the immortal God for images resembling mortal man and birds and animals and creeping things. Therefore God gave them up in the lusts of their hearts to impurity, to the dishonouring of their bodies among themselves, because they exchanged the truth about

27

God for a lie and worshipped and served the creature rather than the Creator, who is blessed forever! Amen...

And since they did not see fit to acknowledge God, God gave them up to a debased mind to do what ought not to be done. They were filled with all manner of unrighteousness, evil, covetousness, malice. They are full of envy, murder, strife, deceit, maliciousness. They are gossips, slanderers, haters of God, insolent, haughty, boastful, inventors of evil, disobedient to parents, foolish, faithless, heartless, ruthless. Though they know God's righteous decree that those who practice such things deserve to die, they not only do them but give approval to those who practice them (Rom. 1:18-32).

Let me take the liberty of putting the apostle's words into the present tense:

By their unrighteousness, the unregenerate suppress the truth... They do not honour God as God or give thanks to him, but they become futile in their thinking, and their foolish hearts are darkened. Claiming to be wise, they become fools, and exchange the glory of the immortal God for images... They exchange the truth about God for a lie and worship and serve the creature rather than the Creator... They do not see fit to acknowledge God... [They have] a debased mind... They are full of envy, murder, strife, deceit, maliciousness.

This is the condition of every man or woman by nature; every human being is in this appalling state,[13] in this condition from conception. This is what David meant when he confessed:

I know my transgressions and my sin is ever before me... Behold, I was brought forth in iniquity, and in sin did my mother conceive me (Ps. 51:3-5).

As Eliphaz put it to Job:

What is man, that he can be pure? Or he who is born of a woman, that he can be righteous? (Job 15:14).

The Psalmist declared:

---

[13] In order not to extend this booklet, I simply state that Christ – by virtue of his virgin birth – is the only exception.

The wicked are estranged from the womb; they go astray from birth (Ps. 58:3).

Getting back to where we left off in Romans, as Paul went on to show, all men without exception stand guilty and condemned before God (Rom. 2:1 – 3:23). In short:

> None is righteous, no, not one; no one understands; no one seeks for God... For all have sinned and fall short of the glory of God (Rom. 3:10-11,23).

That is, all of us have sinned in Adam and are thus constituted sinners. We demonstrate this by committing our own sins. As Paul reminded the believers at Ephesus:

> You were dead in the trespasses and sins in which you once walked, following the course of this world, following the prince of the power of the air, the spirit that is now at work in the sons of disobedience – among whom we all once lived in the passions of our flesh, carrying out the desires of the body and the mind, and were by nature children of wrath, like the rest of mankind (Eph. 2:1-3).

Referring to natural men, speaking of 'the futility of their minds', the apostle declared:

> They are darkened in their understanding, alienated from the life of God because of the ignorance that is in them, due to their hardness of heart. They have become callous and have given themselves up to sensuality, greedy to practice every kind of impurity (Eph. 4:17-19).

As he reminded Titus:

> We ourselves were once foolish, disobedient, led astray, slaves to various passions and pleasures, passing our days in malice and envy, hated by others and hating one another (Tit. 3:3).

Here is the merest sample of relevant scriptures making the same point:

> The hearts of the children of man are full of evil, and madness is in their hearts while they live, and after that they go to the dead (Eccles. 9:3).

Can the Ethiopian change his skin or the leopard his spots? Then also you can do good who are accustomed to do evil (Jer. 13:23).

The heart is deceitful above all things, and desperately sick; who can understand it? (Jer. 17:9).

What comes out of a person is what defiles him. For from within, out of the heart of man, come evil thoughts, sexual immorality, theft, murder, adultery, coveting, wickedness, deceit, sensuality, envy, slander, pride, foolishness. All these evil things come from within, and they defile a person (Mark. 7:20-23).

None are exempt:

Everyone who commits sin is a slave of sin (John 8:34).

It is appointed for man to die once, and after that comes judgment (Heb. 9:27).

The whole world lies in the power of the evil one (1 John 5:19).

This is how Adam left the human race. This is what man's ruin means. Everyone of us is born in this condition.

No wonder, then, as Christ told Nicodemus:

Truly, truly, I say to you, unless one is born again he cannot see the kingdom of God... Truly, truly, I say to you, unless one is born of water and the Spirit, he cannot enter the kingdom of God. That which is born of the flesh is flesh, and that which is born of the Spirit is spirit. Do not marvel that I said to you: 'You must be born again' (John 3:3-7).

Nothing less will do!

As Joseph Hoskins put it:

> *Sinners! this solemn truth regard;*
> *Hear, all you sons of men!*
> *For Christ the Saviour has declared:*
> *'You must be born again'.*

Man's Ruin

Whate'er might be your birth or blood,
The sinner's boast is vain;
Thus says the glorious Son of God:
'You must be born again'.

Our nature totally depraved,
The heart a sink of sin;
Without a change we can't be saved,
'You must be born again'.

That which is born of flesh is flesh,
And flesh it will remain:
Then marvel not that Jesus says:
'You must be born again'.

This is the need. Is there any hope of it?

Man's Redemption

Adam sinned and by his fall constituted all his descendants sinners. This means that all men are ruined in Adam, dead in sin, unable to put the matter right.

Consequently, the great question must be this: How can man be rescued, redeemed, delivered from this appalling condition?

The biblical answer is clear. Man can only be put right with God by God's direct intervention.

What is this 'direct intervention'?

God sent his Son into the world to accomplish redemption for sinners. Hence the great, triumphant cry of the Lord Jesus in his death: 'It is finished' (John 19:30); that is: 'It is accomplished!' Christ had come into the world to do his Father's will (Heb. 10:4-10), and that will was to save his elect (Matt. 1:21; 1 Tim. 1:15, for instance): 'By that will [that is, by Christ's obedience to his Father's will] we [that is, the elect] have been sanctified through the offering of the body of Jesus Christ once for all' (Heb. 10:10); in other words, Christ has redeemed his elect.

Thus, Paul writing to the Corinthians, could state:

> For as by a man came death, by a man has come also the resurrection of the dead. For as in Adam all [that is, all who are in Adam – all men] die, so also in Christ shall all [that is, all who are in Christ – the elect] be made alive (1 Cor. 15:21-22).

> The first man Adam became a living being; the last Adam became a life-giving spirit. But it is not the spiritual that is first but the natural, and then the spiritual. The first man was from the earth, a man of dust; the second man is from heaven. As was the man of dust, so also are those who are of the dust, and as is the man of heaven, so also are those who are of heaven. Just as we [the apostle is now speaking of

33

believers] have borne the image of the man of dust, we shall also bear the image of the man of heaven (1 Cor. 15:45-49).

With that as a kind of preface, let me now pick up where we left off with Paul's words to the Romans – at the point where the apostle is comparing – or, rather, contrasting – the works and accomplishments of Adam and Christ:

> ...sin came into the world through one man, [that is, Adam] and death through sin, and so death spread to all men because all sinned... But the free gift is not like the trespass. For if many [that is, all in Adam] died through one man's trespass, much more have the grace of God and the free gift by the grace of that one man Jesus Christ abounded for many [that is, the elect]. And the free gift is not like the result of that one man's sin. For the judgment following one trespass brought condemnation, but the free gift following many trespasses brought justification. For if, because of one man's trespass, death reigned through that one man, much more will those who receive the abundance of grace and the free gift of righteousness reign in life through the one man Jesus Christ. Therefore, as one trespass led to condemnation for all men [who are in Adam; that is, all men], so one act of righteousness leads to justification and life for all men [who are in Christ; that is, the elect]. For as by the one man's disobedience the many were made sinners, so by the one man's obedience the many will be made righteous. Now the law came in to increase the trespass, but where sin increased, grace abounded all the more, so that, as sin reigned in death, grace also might reign through righteousness leading to eternal life through Jesus Christ our Lord (Rom. 5:12-21).

In short, as all who are in Adam – every human being – fell into sin and under condemnation with Adam, so all who are in Christ – the elect – were redeemed in and through the sacrifice of Christ.

This, in brief, is what I meant by 'God's direct intervention'.

Of course, there is much more that needs to be said about all this. When exactly are the elect justified? What, precisely, is the righteousness that is imputed to believers? Such major questions are only two of the many which need to be answered, but, trying be brief in this booklet, and since I have dealt with both elsewhere,[14] I simply state that while the elect were justified in God's decree in eternity past, and were justified by Christ in his death and resurrection, and will be finally and fully justified in eternity to come, they are actually justified as they come to saving trust in Christ – and actually only then:

The righteousness of God has been manifested... the righteousness of God through faith in Jesus Christ for all who believe. For there is no distinction: for all have sinned and fall short of the glory of God, and are justified by his grace as a gift, through the redemption that is in Christ Jesus, whom God put forward as a propitiation by his blood, to be received by faith. This was to show God's righteousness, because in his divine forbearance he had passed over former sins. It was to show his righteousness at the present time, so that he might be just and the justifier of the one who has faith in Jesus (Rom. 3:21-26).

Therefore, since we have been justified by faith, we have peace with God through our Lord Jesus Christ. Through him we have also obtained access by faith into this grace in which we stand, and we rejoice in hope of the glory of God... God's love has been poured into our hearts through the Holy Spirit who has been given to us. For while we were still weak, at the right time Christ died for the ungodly. For one will scarcely die for a righteous person – though perhaps for a good person one would dare even to die – but God shows his love for us in that while we were still sinners, Christ died for us. Since, therefore, we have now been justified by his blood, much more shall we be saved by him from the wrath of God. For if while we were enemies we were reconciled to God by the death of his Son, much more, now that we are reconciled, shall we be saved by his life. More than that, we also rejoice in God through our Lord Jesus Christ, through whom we have now received reconciliation (Rom. 5:1-11).

And so to Romans 5:12-21, already quoted.

---

[14] See my *Eternal*; *Imputed*.

In a parallel passage to Romans 5, when writing to the Ephesians, Paul makes the same point. Having set out the sinner's (including the elect sinner's) natural condition:

> You were dead in the trespasses and sins in which you once walked, following the course of this world, following the prince of the power of the air, the spirit that is now at work in the sons of disobedience – among whom we all once lived in the passions of our flesh, carrying out the desires of the body and the mind, and were by nature children of wrath, like the rest of mankind (Eph. 2:1-3)...

...the apostle moves on to the remedy:

> But God, being rich in mercy, because of the great love with which he loved us [that is, the elect], even when we were dead in our trespasses, made us alive together with Christ – by grace you have been saved – and raised us up with him and seated us with him in the heavenly places in Christ Jesus, so that in the coming ages he might show the immeasurable riches of his grace in kindness toward us in Christ Jesus. For by grace you have been saved through faith. And this is not your own doing; it is the gift of God, not a result of works, so that no one may boast. For we are his workmanship, created in Christ Jesus for good works, which God prepared beforehand, that we should walk in them (Eph. 2:4-10).

Here we have the way of redemption. Everyone of us is born a sinner, dead in sin, under the wrath of God. But – what a glorious word[15] – God has intervened, sending his Son into the world to redeem his people from their sin. What is more, God does not leave it there: his Spirit applies the finished work of Christ to the elect – regenerating them, convicting them of sin, bringing them to repentance and saving faith in Christ. All is on the basis of God's grace, love, kindness and mercy.

---

[15] Take the phrase 'but now' (Rom. 3:21-22. 5:9,11; 6:22; 7:6; 8:1; 11:30; 11:31 (second 'now' in NIV, NASB); 16:26; along with John 15:22,24; Acts 17:30; 1 Cor. 15:20; Gal. 4:9; Eph. 2:12-13; 5:8; Col. 1:26; Heb. 8:6; 9:26; 12:26; 1 Pet. 2:10). For more on this, see my *Christ*; *Public*.

Salvation does not stop at mere deliverance from the guilt and condemnation of sin; it includes the deliverance of the believer from the power of sin, displayed in his life-long growth in grace in obedience to Christ in the manifestation of good works, produced by the energy and power of the Holy Spirit – good works, not to obtain salvation, but good works produced by those who live in gratitude and obedience to the God who has saved them.

Scripture never tires of the theme:

> Thanks be to God, that you who were once slaves of sin have become obedient from the heart to the standard of teaching to which you were committed, and, having been set free from sin, have become slaves of righteousness. I am speaking in human terms, because of your natural limitations. For just as you once presented your members as slaves to impurity and to lawlessness leading to more lawlessness, so now present your members as slaves to righteousness leading to sanctification.
> For when you were slaves of sin, you were free in regard to righteousness. But what fruit were you getting at that time from the things of which you are now ashamed? For the end of those things is death. But now that you have been set free from sin and have become slaves of God, the fruit you get leads to sanctification and its end, eternal life. For the wages of sin is death, but the free gift of God is eternal life in Christ Jesus our Lord (Rom. 6:17-23).

> The Lord Jesus Christ... gave himself for our sins to deliver us from the present evil age, according to the will of our God and Father (Gal. 1:3-4).

> The grace of God has appeared, bringing salvation for all people, training us to renounce ungodliness and worldly passions, and to live self-controlled, upright, and godly lives in the present age, waiting for our blessed hope, the appearing of the glory of our great God and Saviour Jesus Christ, who gave himself for us to redeem us from all lawlessness and to purify for himself a people for his own possession who are zealous for good works... We ourselves were once foolish, disobedient, led astray, slaves to various passions and pleasures, passing our days in malice and envy, hated by others and hating one another. But when the

goodness and loving kindness of God our Saviour appeared, he saved us, not because of works done by us in righteousness, but according to his own mercy, by the washing of regeneration and renewal of the Holy Spirit, whom he poured out on us richly through Jesus Christ our Saviour, so that being justified by his grace we might become heirs according to the hope of eternal life (Tit. 2:11 – 3:7).

To him who loves us and has freed us from our sins by his blood and made us a kingdom, priests to his God and Father, to him be glory and dominion forever and ever. Amen (Rev. 1:5-6).

This is man's redemption.

Conclusion

Having sketched an outline of man's uniqueness, man's ruin and man's redemption, I have finished my task.

Or have I?

Far from it!

As I explained, I am a preacher. My task, my responsibility, my privilege is to seek to persuade as many of my fellow-men and women as I can to know feel and enjoy the experience of redemption by Christ. In short, I have published this booklet in the hope that you, reader, might come to know that, though you were born dead in sin, you can be redeemed through the blood and righteousness of the Lord Jesus Christ. I go further: I want you not only to know that you can be redeemed by trusting Christ, I want to do what I can to persuade you to trust Christ and so be redeemed from your sin. Scripture assures you that if you do trust Christ you will be saved:

> I, the LORD... there is no other God besides me, a righteous God and a Saviour; there is none besides me. 'Turn to me and be saved, all the ends of the earth! For I am God, and there is no other' (Isa. 45:21-22).

As Jesus said:

> Come to me, all who labour and are heavy laden, and I will give you rest. Take my yoke upon you, and learn from me, for I am gentle and lowly in heart, and you will find rest for your souls. For my yoke is easy, and my burden is light (Matt. 11:28-30).

You may rest assured that if you trust Christ you will be saved:

> Believe on the Lord Jesus, and you will be saved (Acts 16:31).

... everyone who calls on the name of the Lord will be saved (Rom. 10:13).

So:

Seek the LORD while he may be found; call upon him while he is near (Isa. 55:6).

In Christ God was reconciling the world to himself, not counting their trespasses against them, and entrusting to us the message of reconciliation. Therefore, we are ambassadors for Christ, God making his appeal through us. We implore you on behalf of Christ, be reconciled to God. For our sake he made him to be sin who knew no sin, so that in him we might become the righteousness of God. Working together with him, then, we appeal to you not to receive the grace of God in vain... Behold, now is the favourable time; behold, now is the day of salvation (2 Cor. 5:19 – 6:2).

Printed in Great Britain
by Amazon

73280941R00031